United States Presidents

Millard Fillmore

Paul Joseph

ABDO Publishing Company

visit us at
www.abdopub.com

Published by Abdo Publishing Company 4940 Viking Drive, Edina, Minnesota 55435.
Copyright © 1999 by Abdo Consulting Group, Inc. International copyrights reserved in
all countries. No part of this book may be reproduced in any form without written
permission from the publisher.

Printed in the United States.

Cover and Interior Photo credits: AP/Wide World, Archive, Corbis-Bettmann

Contributing editors: Robert Italia, Tamara L. Britton, K. M. Brielmaier
Book design/maps: Patrick Laurel

Library of Congress Cataloging-in-Publication Data

Joseph, Paul, 1970-
    Millard Fillmore / Paul Joseph.
       p. cm. -- (United States presidents)
    Includes index.
    Summary: Examines the life of the president who helped postpone
the Civil War with the Compromise of 1850 and who was
considered to have destroyed his political career in order to
preserve the Union.
    ISBN 1-57765-235-5
    1. Fillmore, Millard, 1800-1874--Juvenile literature. 2. Presidents
--United States--Biography--Juvenile literature. [1. Fillmore, Millard, 1800-
1874. 2. Presidents.] I. title. II. Series: United States presidents (Edina,
Minn.)
E427.J67 1999
973.6'4'092--dc21
    [B]
                                       98-16241
                                       CIP
                                       AC

Contents

Millard Fillmore 4

Young Millard 8

Family Man and Politics 10

Vice President Fillmore 12

The Making of the Thirteenth
       United States President 14

The Thirteenth President.................................. 16

The Seven "Hats" of the U.S President 18

The Three Branches of the U.S. Government... 19

Trouble in the Country 20

After the White House 24

Buffalo 26

Fun Facts.. 28

Glossary 30

Internet Sites 31

Index 32

Millard Fillmore

*M*illard Fillmore was the thirteenth president of the United States. He led the country through one of the worst times in American history. The North and the South argued about slavery. Later, these arguments led to the **Civil War**.

In 1828, Fillmore began to work in politics. He was elected to the New York state **legislature**. Four years later, he was elected to **Congress.**

In 1848, Zachary Taylor was elected president. Fillmore was elected vice president. Just 16 months later, President Taylor died. By law, Fillmore became the next president.

Fillmore led the country through a tough time. He helped pass the Compromise of 1850. He thought the Compromise would solve the slavery problem. But neither the North nor the South liked the new laws. President Fillmore was so unpopular, he did not run for re-election.

Millard Fillmore did what he thought was right for the country. He began his journey to the White House on a New York farm.

Millard Fillmore

Millard Fillmore (1800-1874)
Thirteenth President

BORN:	January 7, 1800
PLACE OF BIRTH:	Locke (Cayuga County) New York
ANCESTRY:	English
FATHER:	Nathaniel Fillmore (1771-1863)
MOTHER:	Phoebe Millard Fillmore (1780-1831)
WIVES:	First wife: Abigail Powers (1798-1853)
	Second wife: Caroline Carmichael McIntosh (1813-1881)
CHILDREN:	Two: 1 boy, 1 girl (by first wife)
EDUCATION:	Attended public schools; studied law in Cayuga County and Buffalo, New York
RELIGION:	Unitarian
OCCUPATION:	Lawyer, teacher, congressman
MILITARY SERVICE:	None
POLITICAL PARTY:	Whig

OFFICES HELD: Member of New York legislature; member of U.S. House of Representatives; New York State comptroller; vice president

AGE AT INAUGURATION: 50

YEARS SERVED: 1850-1853

VICE PRESIDENT: None

DIED: March 8, 1874, Buffalo, New York, age 74

CAUSE OF DEATH: Stroke

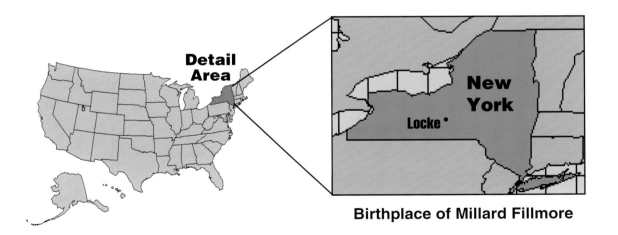

Detail Area

New York

Locke

Birthplace of Millard Fillmore

Young Millard

*M*illard Fillmore was born in a log cabin in Locke, Cayuga County, New York, on January 7, 1800. He was the second child born to Nathaniel and Phoebe Fillmore.

As a boy, Millard worked on the family farm. Because he worked so much, he went to school only three months each year. His mother taught Millard at home. He learned reading, writing, and arithmetic.

When Millard was 14 years old, he became an **apprentice** wool worker. He agreed to work for seven years. After five years, he paid his employer to free him from the agreement.

When he was 19, Millard moved to Montville, New York. He found a job in a law office. Millard did not spend much time in school. But he was smart and loved to read. He got a part-time job teaching school.

Fillmore became a lawyer in 1823. For seven years, he practiced law in East Aurora, New York.

In 1830, Fillmore moved his law firm to Buffalo, New York. His business grew. In a few years, his law practice was one of the best known in the state.

Millard Fillmore as a young man

Family Man and Politics

*I*n 1826, Fillmore married Abigail Powers of Moravia, New York. Abigail was born in Stillwater, New York, in 1798. Millard and Abigail first met in 1819. The Fillmores had two children, Millard Powers in 1828, and Mary Abigail in 1832.

In 1828, Fillmore began to work in politics. He was elected to the New York **legislature**. In 1832, Fillmore was elected to **Congress**. He moved to Washington, D.C.

In 1834, Fillmore joined the **Whig party**. As a Whig, he helped make laws that taxed goods from other

Abigail Powers Fillmore

10

countries. These high taxes made it hard for other countries to sell things like food and clothes in America. United States businesses sold more goods to Americans. The economy improved. Fillmore and the **Whig party** grew popular.

As a congressman, Fillmore supported new inventions and businesses. He helped Samuel F. B. Morse develop the telegraph. It helped Americans **communicate** with each other.

Samuel Morse

Vice President Fillmore

*I*n 1844, Fillmore ran for governor of New York. He lost a close election. Fillmore did not give up on politics. In 1847, he was elected the state comptroller to handle New York's money.

In 1848, the **Whig party** chose Zachary Taylor to run for president. The party chose Fillmore to run for vice president. Taylor was a Southerner. Fillmore was a Northerner. They appealed to many Americans, and won the election.

As vice president, Fillmore ran the Senate meetings. The Senate argued about slavery. Fillmore insisted that the senators respect each other. He brought order to the Senate.

Opposite page:
President Zachary Taylor

The Making of the Thirteenth United States President

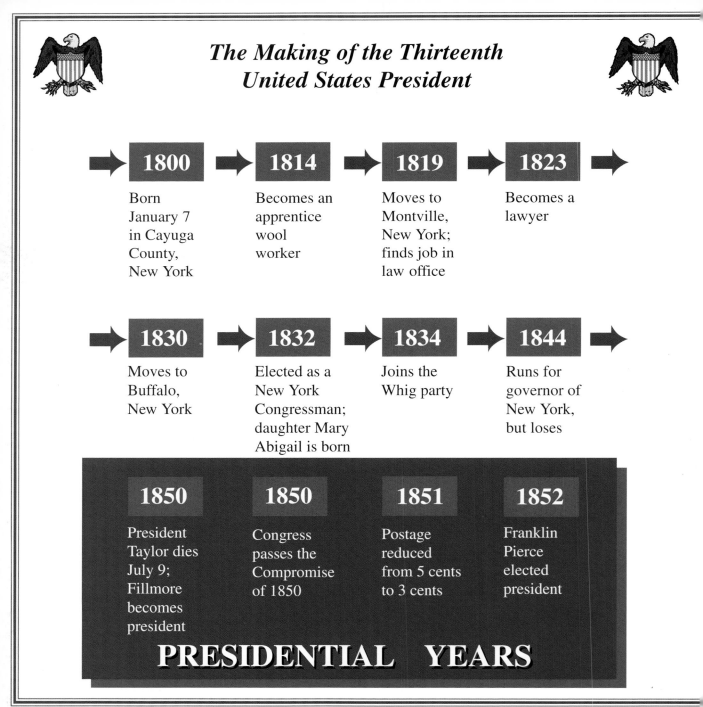

1800 Born January 7 in Cayuga County, New York

1814 Becomes an apprentice wool worker

1819 Moves to Montville, New York; finds job in law office

1823 Becomes a lawyer

1830 Moves to Buffalo, New York

1832 Elected as a New York Congressman; daughter Mary Abigail is born

1834 Joins the Whig party

1844 Runs for governor of New York, but loses

1850 President Taylor dies July 9; Fillmore becomes president

1850 Congress passes the Compromise of 1850

1851 Postage reduced from 5 cents to 3 cents

1852 Franklin Pierce elected president

PRESIDENTIAL YEARS

Millard Fillmore

*"The Constitution has made it the duty of the President
to take care that the laws be faithfully executed."*

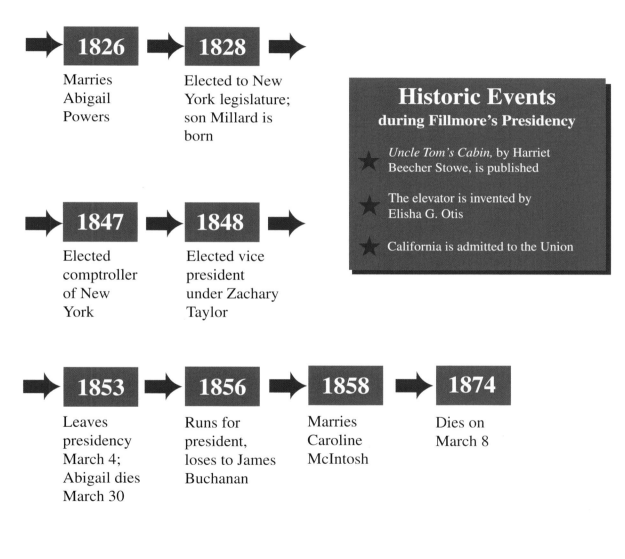

1826
Marries
Abigail
Powers

1828
Elected to New
York legislature;
son Millard is
born

Historic Events
during Fillmore's Presidency

★ *Uncle Tom's Cabin*, by Harriet
Beecher Stowe, is published

★ The elevator is invented by
Elisha G. Otis

★ California is admitted to the Union

1847
Elected
comptroller
of New
York

1848
Elected vice
president
under Zachary
Taylor

1853
Leaves
presidency
March 4;
Abigail dies
March 30

1856
Runs for
president,
loses to James
Buchanan

1858
Marries
Caroline
McIntosh

1874
Dies on
March 8

The Thirteenth President

While Millard Fillmore was vice president, the Senate **debated** the Compromise of 1850. Kentucky senator Henry Clay proposed these laws to end the slavery arguments.

The Compromise said that the new state of California could forbid slavery. It banned slave trading in Washington, D.C. It also said that the new territories of New Mexico and Utah could allow slavery if they wanted to.

The Compromise included the Fugitive Slave Act. Runaway slaves could be captured and returned to their masters. Northerners who hid runaway slaves could go to jail.

President Taylor was against the Compromise. But on July 9, 1850, he died. By law, Vice President Fillmore became president.

President Fillmore supported the Compromise of 1850. He believed that without these new laws, a **civil war** would start. Then the United States would break apart. Fillmore wanted to

The Compromise of 1850

Free State or Territory

Utah Territory

California

New Mexico Territory

Slave State or Territory

settle the slavery problem. Two months later, **Congress** passed the Compromise of 1850. President Fillmore was sure that the slavery problem was solved.

President Fillmore also worked for trading rights with other countries. He sent Commodore Matthew Perry to form a treaty with Japan. This treaty opened Japanese ports to U.S. ships. The United States profited from Japan.

The Seven "Hats" of the U.S. President

A president can serve only two terms. Each term lasts four years. When Fillmore was president, this law did not exist.

A president is elected or re-elected every four years.

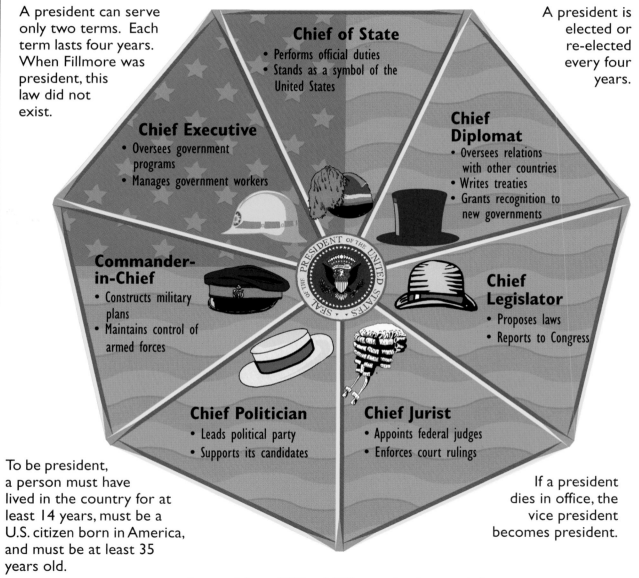

Chief of State
- Performs official duties
- Stands as a symbol of the United States

Chief Executive
- Oversees government programs
- Manages government workers

Chief Diplomat
- Oversees relations with other countries
- Writes treaties
- Grants recognition to new governments

Commander-in-Chief
- Constructs military plans
- Maintains control of armed forces

Chief Legislator
- Proposes laws
- Reports to Congress

Chief Politician
- Leads political party
- Supports its candidates

Chief Jurist
- Appoints federal judges
- Enforces court rulings

To be president, a person must have lived in the country for at least 14 years, must be a U.S. citizen born in America, and must be at least 35 years old.

If a president dies in office, the vice president becomes president.

As president, Millard Fillmore had seven jobs.

The Three Branches of the U.S. Government

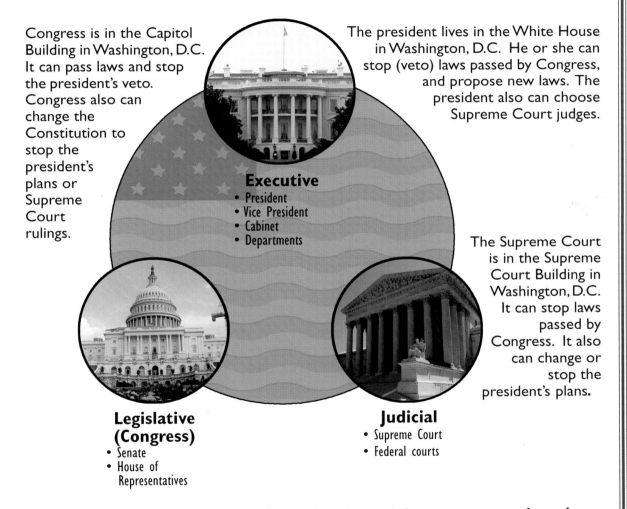

Congress is in the Capitol Building in Washington, D.C. It can pass laws and stop the president's veto. Congress also can change the Constitution to stop the president's plans or Supreme Court rulings.

The president lives in the White House in Washington, D.C. He or she can stop (veto) laws passed by Congress, and propose new laws. The president also can choose Supreme Court judges.

Executive
- President
- Vice President
- Cabinet
- Departments

The Supreme Court is in the Supreme Court Building in Washington, D.C. It can stop laws passed by Congress. It also can change or stop the president's plans.

Legislative (Congress)
- Senate
- House of Representatives

Judicial
- Supreme Court
- Federal courts

The U.S. Constitution was written in 1787. It formed three government branches. Each branch has power over the others. So, no single group or person can control the country. The Constitution calls this "separation of powers."

Trouble in the Country

*P*resident Fillmore spent most of his time dealing with the slavery problem. The Compromise of 1850 was not working. Americans still fought over slavery. The Fugitive Slave Act was the biggest problem.

In 1851, 20 escaped slaves arrived in Christina, Pennsylvania. Their owner soon came from the South to catch them. A gunfight broke out between the slaves and the owner. The slave owner died. The slaves were arrested.

Northerners were angry. They felt the slaves were only defending themselves. After a trial, the slaves were declared innocent.

Now, Southerners were angry. President Fillmore was not enforcing the Compromise of 1850. He was caught between the North and the South. Neither side was happy with him.

The United States during Fillmore's Presidency (1850-1853)

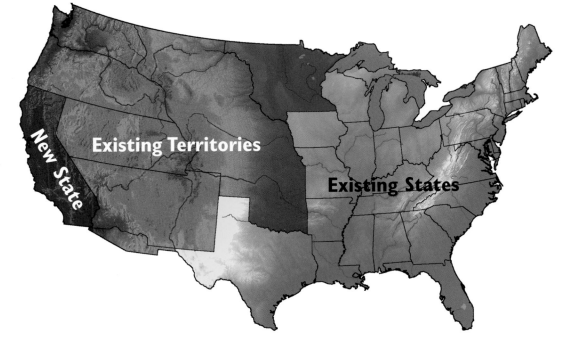

That year, 2,000 people broke into a courthouse in Syracuse, New York. They freed a runaway slave. Southerners demanded that President Fillmore enforce the law. But he did not. This made the South even more angry. The president's popularity continued to fall.

Fillmore believed the Compromise of 1850 would keep the United States together. But it was pulling the country apart. By 1861, 11 states would leave the Union. They would form the **Confederate States of America**.

Kentucky senator Henry Clay wrote the Compromise of 1850.

America during the Civil War (1863)

The United States of America

The Confederate States of America

After the White House

*N*orthern **Whigs** did not choose Millard Fillmore to run for president in 1852. Fillmore knew he would not be chosen. When he signed the Compromise of 1850, he knew that it would make the Northern Whigs unhappy.

The Whigs chose General Winfield Scott to run for president. They hoped that Scott could unite the Whig party and win the election.

The Whigs lost the election to **Democrat** Franklin Pierce. As a political party, the Whigs were almost finished. Millard Fillmore was the last Whig president in U.S. history.

Fillmore left the White House on March 4, 1853. Twenty-six days later, Abigail died of **pneumonia**.

Fillmore was greatly saddened by the death of his wife. A year later, his daughter Mary died suddenly. Fillmore was heartbroken. To keep busy, he returned to politics.

But politics was changing. Between 1845 and 1855, nearly three million people arrived in the U.S. from other countries. In the 1840s, a secret group formed that wanted to pass laws against these newcomers. The people in this group called themselves the Know-Nothings. Soon the Know-Nothings formed a new political party. They called it the American Party.

But the **Democratic** party supported people from other countries. So, most of the new Americans became Democrats.

Mary Abigail Fillmore

Buffalo

*M*illard Fillmore decided to run for president again. He ran for the American Party. In November 1856, he lost to **Democrat** James Buchanan. After this loss, Fillmore left politics for good. But he continued to support other politicians.

Fillmore moved to Buffalo, New York. In 1858, he married Caroline McIntosh. Caroline and Millard had many friends. They enjoyed spending time with them.

Fillmore's 1856 election banner

MILLARD FILLMORE,

Fillmore did much for Buffalo. He represented the Buffalo Board of Trade. He supported the city's libraries. He became the first **chancellor** of the University of Buffalo. And he helped start a hospital.

In 1862, Fillmore became the first president of the Buffalo Historical Society. In 1867, he helped start a social club called the Buffalo Club. Fillmore greeted many important visitors to the city.

Fillmore spent his last years close to his wife, who was ill. He suffered a stroke on February 13, 1874. Two weeks later, he had another attack. He died on March 8.

Slavery divided the nation while Fillmore was president. He tried his best to solve this problem with wisdom and laws. But only a war could save the Union.

The Buffalo Historical Society

Fun Facts

- Millard Fillmore was the first president to have a bathtub in the White House.

- The Fillmores bought the first kitchen stove for the White House. The White House cook couldn't figure out how to use it, so President Fillmore took a class and taught the cook.

- Abigail Fillmore started the White House Library. When the Fillmores got to the White House, there were no books. When they left, there were hundreds.

- Millard Fillmore was the first president to have a stepmother.

- When Oxford University wanted to give President Fillmore an honorary **degree**, he refused it. The degree was written in Latin. President Fillmore said, "No man should, in my judgment, accept a degree he cannot read."

Millard Fillmore

Glossary

apprentice - a person who learns a trade from a skilled worker.

chancellor - a very high official.

Civil War - a war between groups within the same country. The United States fought a civil war from 1861 to 1865 over slavery.

communicate - to give or exchange information or news.

Confederate States of America - the country formed by the 11 southern states that left the Union between 1860 and 1861.

Congress - the lawmaking body of the U.S. government. It is made up of the Senate and the House of Representatives.

debate - a public discussion of reasons for or against something.

degree - a title given by a college to its graduates, or to honor a famous person.

Democrat - one of the two main political parties in the United States. Democrats are often more liberal and believe in more government.

legislature - the lawmaking group of a state or country.

pneumonia - a disease that causes difficult breathing and a high fever.

Whig party - a political group that was very strong in the early 1800s, but ended in the 1850s. They supported laws that helped business.

Internet Sites

PBS American Presidents Series
http://www.americanpresidents.org
Visit the PBS Web site which features the biographies of each president. Check out the key events of each presidency, speeches, fun facts, and trivia games.

Welcome to the White House
http://www.whitehouse.gov
The official Web site of the White House. After an introduction from the current president of the United States, the site takes you through biographies of each president. Get information on White House history, art in the White House, first ladies, first families, and much more.

POTUS—Presidents of the United States
http://www.ipl.org/ref/POTUS/
In this Web site you will find background information, election results, cabinet members, presidency highlights, and some odd facts on each of the presidents. Links to biographies, historical documents, audio and video files, and other presidential sites are also included to enrich this site.

These sites are subject to change. Go to your favorite search engine and type in United States presidents for more sites.

Pass It On

History enthusiasts: educate readers around the country by passing on information you've learned about presidents or other important people who have changed history. Share your little-known facts and interesting stories. We want to hear from you!

To get posted on the ABDO Publishing Company Web site, email us at "History@abdopub.com"
Visit the ABDO Publishing Company Web site at www.abdopub.com

Index

A
American Party 25, 26
apprentice 8

B
birth 8
Buchanan, James 26
Buffalo, New York 9, 26, 27
Buffalo Club 27
Buffalo Historical Society 27

C
California 16
chancellor 27
children 10, 24, 25
Civil War 4, 27
Clay, Henry 16
Compromise of 1850 4, 16, 17, 20, 22, 24
Confederate States of America 22
Congress, U.S. 4, 10, 17
congressman 11

D
death 27
Democratic party 24, 25, 26

E
election 10, 12, 24, 26

F
farm 8
Fugitive Slave Act 16, 20

G
governor 12

J
Japan 17
jobs 8

K
Know-Nothings 25

L
lawyer 9
legislature 4, 10

M
marriage 10, 26
Morse, Samuel F. B. 11

N
New Mexico 16
New York Legislature 10

P
parents 8
Perry, Matthew 17
Pierce, Franklin 24
president 4, 16, 17, 20, 22, 24, 26, 27, 28

R
re-election 4, 24, 26

S
school 8
Scott, Winfield 24
Senate, U.S. 12, 16
slavery 4, 16, 17, 20, 22, 27
state comptroller 12
Syracuse, New York 22

T
taxes 11
Taylor, Zachary 4, 12, 16
telegraph 11
territories 16

U
University of Buffalo 27
Utah 16

V
vice president 4, 12, 16

W
Washington, D.C. 10, 16
Whig party 10, 11, 12, 24
White House 5, 24, 28
White House Library 28
wives 10, 24, 26, 27, 28